Common Core Lessons & Activities:

Forms of Government:

Democracy, Monarchy, Dictatorship & More

By Carole Marsh

Published by Gallopade International, Inc.

Printed in the U.S.A. (Peachtree City, Georgia)

TABLE OF CONTENTS

G: Includes Graphic Organizer

GO: Graphic Organizer is also available 8½" x 11" online download at www.gallopade.com/client/go

(numbers above correspond to the graphic organizer numbers online)

What Is Government?

Read the text and answer the questions.

There are approximately 196 countries in the world. They are different sizes and shapes, and have different climates, natural resources, and people. However, every country has some form of government. A government is a system by which a country, state, or community is governed or ruled.

Within each country, state, or community, important decisions have to be made. Who leads the country? What laws do citizens have to obey? What should students learn in school? Who pays taxes and how should they be paid? Who decides when the country should go to war? A government answers all of these questions and more.

Although every country has a government, not all governments are the same. Across the world, there are many different "forms of government"—each with a different way of organizing power. For example, in a monarchy, a king or queen makes important laws for the country. He or she typically rules for life and passes power to another member of the royal family. In a democracy, citizens of the country vote on laws and elect their leaders. In an oligarchy, a small group of powerful leaders controls the government and makes the laws.

1. Match the following questions to whether they are best answered by paragraph 1, 2, or 3 of the text.
   A. _____What is the purpose of a government?
   B. _____What is a government?
   C. _____Who has the power in a government?
2. Define government as it is used in the text.
3. A. **True** or **false**: All countries have a government.
   B. Why or why not?
4. List at least three decisions that a government makes.
5. A. In a monarchy, who has the power?
   B. In a democracy, who has the power?
   C. In an oligarchy, who has the power?

CLASSIFYING INFORMATION

Limited & Unlimited Powers

Read the text and answer the questions.

Forms of government around the world are structured (built or organized) in different ways. The structure of a government determines the relationship between those in power and the individual citizens. Because a government has power to make laws, citizens' rights and lives are directly affected by their government.

The structure of a government may give the government unlimited power. When a government has unlimited power, there are no restrictions or controls over what the government can do. The government has absolute power over the citizens' lives. Citizens do not have a way to protect their rights, and are often not allowed to debate, vote, campaign, or participate in government.

The structure of a government may limit the government's power. When a government has limited power, it does NOT have absolute control over the citizens. The citizens have some authority to protect their rights and to limit what the government can do and cannot do. Often, the most important citizens' rights and freedoms are granted and protected in a written constitution. Depending on exactly how their government is structured, citizens may also be able to debate, vote, campaign, or participate in government.

1. What is a synonym of structured as it is used in the text?
2. How does a government's structure affect citizens?
3. Complete the graphic organizer by identifying characteristics of governments with unlimited and limited power.

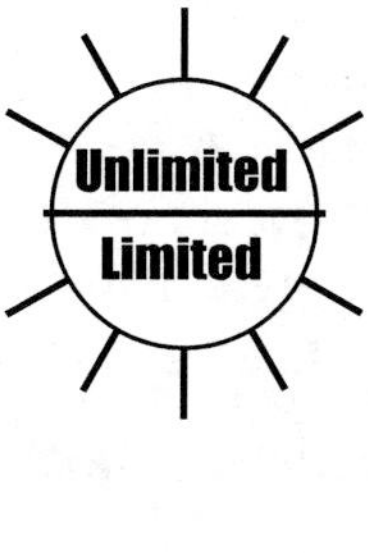

Forms of Government Prefixes & Suffixes

Prefixes are words or letters placed at the beginning of a word to change the meaning. Suffixes are words or letters placed at the end of a word to change the meaning.

PART A: Read the tables and answer the questions.

Prefixes	Meaning
an-	without
aristo-	nobility, wealthy
auto-	self, all-powerful
demo-	people
mon- (mono)	one
olig-	few

Suffixes	Meaning
-archy	rule, or chief ruler
-cracy	power or government

1. Combine prefixes and suffixes to identify the forms of government described in each definition. An example is given below.

Example: Aristocracy — a government that gives power to the wealthy ruling class

A. _______________rule by one person, especially a king or queen
B. _______________a government that gives power to the people
C. _______________rule by a few individuals or a small group of people
D. _______________a government in which one person holds absolute power over all parts of the government
E. _______________without a ruler; chaos and disorder

2. When naming forms of government, what is represented by the prefix? What is represented by the suffix?

PART B: Read the text and use what you have learned from the tables to complete each sentence.

You started the "Clean-Up Kids" club to improve the environment around your school. It is a big success! More than forty students have joined in the first month.

There are lots of decisions to make. When should the group meet? How does the group get the paper and glass to the recycling facility? What kind of flowers should be planted in the school garden? And who will meet with the principal to get permission for future projects?

Another important thing to decide is should you have a constitution, or not? A <u>constitution</u> is a written document that describes the powers of the organization.

The Clean-Up Kids must decide who will be responsible for making the rules and decisions in the club. Once they do that, Clean-Up Kids will have a government to help it run smoothly and effectively.

3. If you alone have absolute control over all parts of the club, your club's government is a/an ______________.
4. If you decide to crown yourself King or Queen of the club and make all other students obey, your club is a/an ________________.
5. You and three of your best friends could run the club as a/an ______________.
6. You could ask all the members to voice their opinions and vote on the best ideas. Then your club would be a/an ________________.
7. You decide that the club should have no leaders and that the club should be a/an _______________.
8. Club members decide they want to write up a list of rules for how the club's power is to be divided and shared in a/an ________________.

PART C: Describe a club, group, or organization in your school. Who makes the rules? Who decides what activities to do? What role do members of the club play? Use what you've learned to identify what form of government best describes the club, group, or organization.

Forms of Democracy

Read the text and answer the questions.

<table>
<tr><td rowspan="2">DEMOCRACY
In a direct democracy, power is held by all citizens. People make decisions and laws for the country by voting. Democracies often have a constitution, or set of laws that outline the powers of the government and the rights or the people.</td><td>DIRECT DEMOCRACY
In a direct democracy, the people directly write the laws that govern their society. All citizens are responsible for voting each time an important decision or law is made.</td></tr>
<tr><td>REPRESENTATIVE DEMOCRACY
In a representative democracy, the citizens vote to elect leaders to government. These leaders are given power from the people to make laws for the public good. These leaders write laws and vote as representatives for the citizens</td></tr>
</table>

1. Why is democracy called a “government by the people”?
2. Who makes the laws in a direct democracy?
   Who makes the laws in a representative democracy?
3. For each item or action listed, identify its purpose in a democracy:

Item / Action	Purpose in a democracy
Voting	
Citizens	
Representatives	
Constitution	

4. Compare and contrast citizens’ participation in a direct democracy to citizens’ participation in a representative democracy.
5. Based on what you know and read, which type of democracy is the United States? Explain your reasoning.
6. Why is it important for citizens to participate in a democracy?

COMPARE & CONTRAST

Athenian & U.S. Democracy

Read the text and answer the questions.

The first democracy developed in the small city-state of Athens, Greece around 550 B.C.E. Citizens gathered together in an outdoor area to argue, debate, and ask questions before voting. Each citizen was allowed one vote. When a majority of voters agreed, a law was passed. To make sure power was shared equally, government leaders were selected at random. All males who were at least 18 years old and owned land were considered citizens and required to vote. Women, children, and slaves were not citizens, and therefore not allowed to vote.

When the Founding Fathers created the United States' government, they included many qualities of the Athenian democracy. However, in the United States, citizens elect representatives to make laws for the country. Citizens also elect a president to perform many roles in leading the nation. Therefore, the United States is called a "presidential democracy."

To limit the government's power, the U.S. government is divided into three branches. Power is shared between elected representatives in the legislative branch, appointed judges in the judicial branch, and the elected president in the executive branch. All citizens of the United States who are at least 18 years old are allowed, but not required, to vote for their elected representatives.

1. A. Who made laws in ancient Athens?
   B. Describe the role of the citizens in ancient Athenian democracy.
   C. Ancient Athens is best described as which form of democracy—direct or representative? Explain why.
2. A. Who makes laws in the United States?
   B. Describe the role of the citizens in the United States democracy.
   C. The United States of America is best described as which form of democracy—direct or representative? Explain why.
3. What is the historical relationship between the government of ancient Athens and the United States government today?
4. List three common characteristics of democracy shared by both Athenian and United States governments.

COMPARE & CONTRAST

Forms of Monarchy

Read the text and answer the questions.

A government may be structured as a monarchy. A monarchy is a form of government that is ruled by one royal ruler, who is called a monarch. Most monarchs are hereditary monarchs, who are given power by being born into the royal family. Hereditary monarchs will later pass their power to their children.

Absolute Monarchy	Constitutional Monarchy
• *The ruler has unlimited power.* • *The rulers may be called a king, queen, or even a sultan or emir.* • *Power is handed down from royal parents to their children.* • *The citizens have no voice in their government.* • *The citizens do not have protected rights.* • *The citizens follow traditions and are loyal to the ruler.*	• *The ruler is primarily a symbol of the government and has no real power.* • *A constitution limits what the ruler can and cannot do.* • *The title of "monarch" is handed down from royal parents to their children.* • *The power to rule is given to a legislature of elected representatives.* • *Citizens have many rights protected by the constitution.* • *Citizens can change the government by electing different representatives.*

1. A. Define monarchy as it is used in the text.
   B. What part of speech is monarch as it is used in the text?
   C. List at least three titles given to monarchs.
2. Which dictionary entry for hereditary (in the box below) best matches the use of the word in the text? Explain.

1) Adj. genetic qualities passed from parent to child
2) Adj. passed from parent to child through a family line
3) Adj. existing by reason of opinion held by family

3. A. Describe the role of a monarch in an absolute monarchy.
   B. Describe the role of a monarch in a constitutional monarchy.
4. Compare and contrast the role of citizens in an absolute monarchy and constitutional monarchy.
5. What can you infer about the purpose of a constitution?

Protecting Citizens' Rights

Many countries have a constitution that protects citizens' rights. The United States Constitution protects the citizen's rights and freedoms, while at the same time limiting the government's use of power.

Read the five paraphrased amendments below. For each, summarize how it limits government and the main rights or freedoms it gives you. One amendment has been completed as an example.

I. The government cannot make laws that limit a person's freedom of speech, freedom to practice any religion, and the freedom to protest peacefully against the government.

II. The government cannot take away the right of a person to carry or use a weapon to defend himself.

III. During peacetime, the government cannot force a person to keep soldiers in his or her home; in wartime, they have to pass a law first.

IV. Citizens have the right to have privacy in home and personal life. No one can search a person's home, body, or things without permission from a judge.

V. A person cannot be charged with a serious crime unless a grand jury says there is enough evidence for a trial. If a jury decides a person is innocent of a crime, that person cannot be tried again with a different jury for the same crime. A person does not have to give evidence against himself unless he wants to confess.

	Limitations on government / Rights and freedoms
I	
II	
III	
IV	
V	This amendment limits the power of judges. I have the right to fair trial in court.

PRIMARY SOURCE ANALYSIS

Monarchs and Peasants

Read the text, look at the painting, and answer the questions.

The first kings of Europe began ruling as wealthy landowners. Poor farmers called <u>*peasants*</u> *worked the land, raised crops, and tended livestock. A king made laws to govern the peasants and trained small armies to defend his land. Peasants were loyal and paid taxes to the king in return for protection from attacks by other kings.*

By taxing the peasants, kings became extremely rich and used the money to increase their armies. These kings used their armies to conquer nearby landowners to expand their kingdoms. When a king died, he passed his land, armies, and power to his children.

1. A. Define <u>peasant</u> as it is used in the text.
   B. Why were peasants loyal to the king?
2. A. List at least two ways kings gained power.
3. A. Who is represented by the person marked by arrow A?
   B. What can you infer about him from his clothes and posture?
4. A. Who is represented by the person marked by arrow B?
   B. What can you infer about him from his clothing and posture?
5. Use what you've learned from the text to create a single-page dialogue between a monarch and peasant. Consider the following questions when creating your dialogue.
   A. Why is the peasant speaking to the king?
   B. How does the king react to the peasant?
   C. Include descriptive details and dialogue that characterize the king as either <u>benevolent</u>* or <u>tyrannical</u>*.

**<u>Benevolent</u>: noun desiring to help others; charitable*

**<u>Tyrannical</u>: noun cruel and oppressive*

CAUSE & EFFECT

Democratic Revolution

Read the text and answer the questions.

In the past, the kings and queens of England, Spain, and France, as well as many other European nations, were absolute monarchs and held great power over their people. Kings often claimed the "divine right of kings," which said a king's rule was given to him by God. Any person who opposed the king was said to oppose God as well.

Over time, citizens of many countries questioned the power of absolute monarchies. In England, the people drafted the Magna Carta, which limited the power of the king and protected citizens' rights. In 1776 during the American Revolution, American colonists declared their freedom from King George III of England. In the French Revolution of 1789, the French people forcefully took control of the government from the king.

These revolutions spread the idea of popular sovereignty across Europe. Popular sovereignty is the idea that government should be controlled by the vote of citizens, not by a single ruler. Many other kings and queens lost power to a form of government that gave power to the people—democracy.

Today, there are no absolute monarchies in the western hemisphere. In a constitutional monarchy, like the United Kingdom, the monarch's power is limited by a constitution. The monarch performs ceremonial duties and is a symbol of the nation, but he or she holds no real power. Citizens hold the power to elect members of Parliament, which makes laws for the country.

1. Why did kings claim that they had "divine right"?
2. For each event, list a direct effect.
   A. The American Revolution
   B. The French Revolution
3. A. Define popular sovereignty as it is used in the text.
   B. How did popular sovereignty affect the monarchies in Europe?
4. A. Describe the role of the monarch in the United Kingdom today.
   B. Who makes laws for the United Kingdom?
5. Which form of government is more democratic—absolute monarchy or constitutional monarchy? Explain.

GRAPHIC ORGANIZER

Government Characteristics

Forms of Government	Rule by One	Rule by Few	Rule by Citizens
Direct Democracy			
Representative Democracy			
Absolute Monarchy			
Constitutional Monarchy			
Dictatorship			
Oligarchy			

Complete the graphic organizer by identifying the characteristics of each form of government listed. Place a ✓ under characteristics that each form of government exhibits. Place an X by characteristics not exhibited by that form of government.

Rule by Representatives	Power is Inherited	Holds Elections for Leaders	Constitutional Government	People Have a Say	Citizens Have Few Rights

INFERENCE

Dictatorship

Read the text and answer the questions.

A government may be structured as a dictatorship. A dictatorship is often described as the opposite of a democracy. Instead of a government ruled by all people, a dictatorship is a government led by one person with overwhelming or absolute power. The kings in some absolute monarchies have been called "dictators" but there is an important difference between a dictator and a king—dictators gain their power by force, not by being born into a royal family.

1. A. Define dictatorship as it is used in the text.
   B. What is the name for the leader of a dictatorship?
2. A. How are dictatorships and absolute monarchies similar?
   B. How are dictatorships and absolute monarchies different?
3. To complete the graphic organizer, rewrite each statement about democracy as its opposite, so it describes a dictatorship.

Democracy	Dictatorship
The government has limited power.	The government has unlimited power.
Government is ruled by all people.	
Citizens have freedom of speech, assembly, religion, and press.	
Citizens have freedom to participate in government.	
Laws are decided by the will of all people.	
Citizens' rights are protected by the government.	

Dictator Quotations

Identify the common theme among the quotations in each column. Then answer the questions.

Adolf Hitler	"What good fortune for governments that the people do not think."	"The very first essential of success is the perpetually constant and regular employment of violence.
Joseph Stalin	"It is enough that the people know there was an election. The people who cast the votes decide nothing. The people who count the votes decide everything."	"Death is the solution to all problems. No man — no problem."
Mao Zedong	"To read too many books is harmful."	"Political power grows out of the barrel of a gun."
Common Theme		

1. What can you infer about the role of the citizens under a dictatorship? Cite evidence from the quotations to support your response.
2. List at least two ways that dictators maintain power over their governments.
3. According to the quotations, what is citizens' most powerful weapon against dictatorship?
4. Use an online resource to research one of the dictators listed in the chart. Write a short oral report telling who they were and what they did. Proofread and edit your report before presenting it to your class.

Forms of Oligarchy

Read the text and answer the questions.

An oligarchy is a government ruled by a small group of powerful people. Depending on which group holds power, each form of oligarchy is given a specific name.

1) "Aristocracy" is the name given to an oligarchy ruled by the wealthiest people. In an aristocracy, the wealthiest people control the government and make rules that poorer citizens must follow. Poorer citizens usually have very few rights and no way of becoming part of the aristocracy.

2) "Theocracy" is the name given to an oligarchy ruled by a group of religious leaders. Religious laws and customs often guide the laws of the government. Under a theocracy, all other religions are usually forbidden. Citizens are not usually allowed to question or change the government law.

3) "Military junta" is a name used to describe an oligarchy ruled by a group of military leaders. These military leaders use the force of the military to rule over the citizens. Citizens live in fear of the military's power.

1. Use the text to write a definition of oligarchy.

2. Complete the graphic organizer by summarizing the main idea of the text and the supporting detail in each paragraph.

Main Idea:	
Paragraph 1	
Paragraph 2	
Paragraph 3	

3. What can you infer about the lives of individual citizens under an oligarchy? Cite evidence from the text to support your inferences.

APPLYING CONCEPTS

Government on the Bus

Read the text and answer the questions.

Imagine you are riding a bus. There are 40 people on the bus including you and the bus driver. You are all citizens of the bus.

1) Imagine that the bus driver is a special person who claims control over all other citizens. The driver acts like royalty, deciding where to go, how to get there, and what speed to drive. He makes rules about where people can sit and who can speak.

2) Soon, 35 of the 40 people believe the driver's rules are unfair and do not like the direction the bus is going. Together, they remove the driver from his position. All citizens then take a vote to elect a new bus driver. Each new rule on the bus is decided by a vote. At an intersection, the bus can either go left or right. Over half of the bus' citizens vote to turn right. Because the <u>majority</u> of the bus's citizens voted to turn right, the driver turns the bus right.

3) After some time, the bus runs low on gasoline. Five people on the bus have all the money. These five wealthy people agree to pay for gasoline. In exchange, they demand that their votes count ten times more than everyone else. Together, the five friends use their unequal voting powers to make new rules for the bus and tell the driver where to go.

1. A. Describe the role of the bus's citizens in section 1.
   B. Describe the role of the bus's citizens in section 2.
   C. Describe the role of the bus's citizens in section 3.
2. Match each of the following forms of government to whether they are best represented by section 1, 2, or 3.
   A. _____ oligarchy B. _____ monarchy C. _____democracy
3. Which form of government gives the most freedom to the citizens? Cite evidence from the text to support your answer.
4. A. Use the text to define the word <u>majority</u>.
   B. What is the role of a majority vote in section 2?
5. List at least two ways the rulers in section 3 maintained power over the people on the bus.

Voter Responsibility

Look at the poster, read the quotations, and answer the questions.

Courtesy of Library of Congress

Democracy cannot succeed unless those who express their choice are prepared to choose wisely. The real safeguard of democracy, therefore, is education.

President Franklin D. Roosevelt

The best argument against democracy is a five-minute conversation with the average voter.

Prime Minister Winston Churchill

1. A. What is the main message of the poster?
   B. What words and symbols helped you to draw your conclusion?
   C. Who is the intended audience of this poster? Cite evidence to support your conclusion.
2. A. Summarize the point of view of President Roosevelt.
   B. According to President Roosevelt, what is a voter's responsibility?
   C. Does President Roosevelt's quotation **support** or **contradict** the poster? Explain your response.
3. A. Summarize the point of view of Prime Minister Churchill.
   B. What is Churchill's opinion of the average voter? Why?
   C. Does Prime Minister Churchill's quotation **support** or **contradict** the poster? Explain your response.
4. In your opinion, is the message of this poster important today? Why or why not? Discuss as a class and expand your response based on the discussion.

More Forms of Government!

Read the definitions and answer the questions below.

Absolute monarchy: complete rule by a king or queen, with no constitution or limits to the ruler's power

Commonwealth: a government of smaller units joined together for the good of the people, similar to a republic

Constitutional monarchy: a monarchy that has been limited by a constitution, giving power to the people to elect representatives and participate in government

Dictatorship: ultimate power of the government rests with one dictator. A dictator often takes power by military force, and takes away the freedoms of some, or all, the people.

Emirate: power is held by an a single "emir," the title of a royal ruler in a Muslim state

Islamic republic: a form of democratic government adopted in some Muslim countries where the government's laws support the laws of the Islamic religion.

Parliamentary democracy: a system where the elected legislative body makes decisions and chooses high government officials

Republic: a democracy in which citizens elect representatives to vote on issues for them. The head of state is an elected president rather than a monarch.

Theocracy: a government where the laws are governed by a religion, and the leader is believed to act for God. Power is often held by a small group of religious leaders

1. Which governments have characteristics of an autocracy?
2. Which forms of government have characteristics of an oligarchy?
3. Which governments have characteristics of a representative democracy?
4. A. How are theocracy and an Islamic republic similar?
   B. How are they different?
5. Which definition best describes the government of the United States? Explain why.

MAP ACTIVITY

Mapping Democracy

Look at the map, and answer the questions.

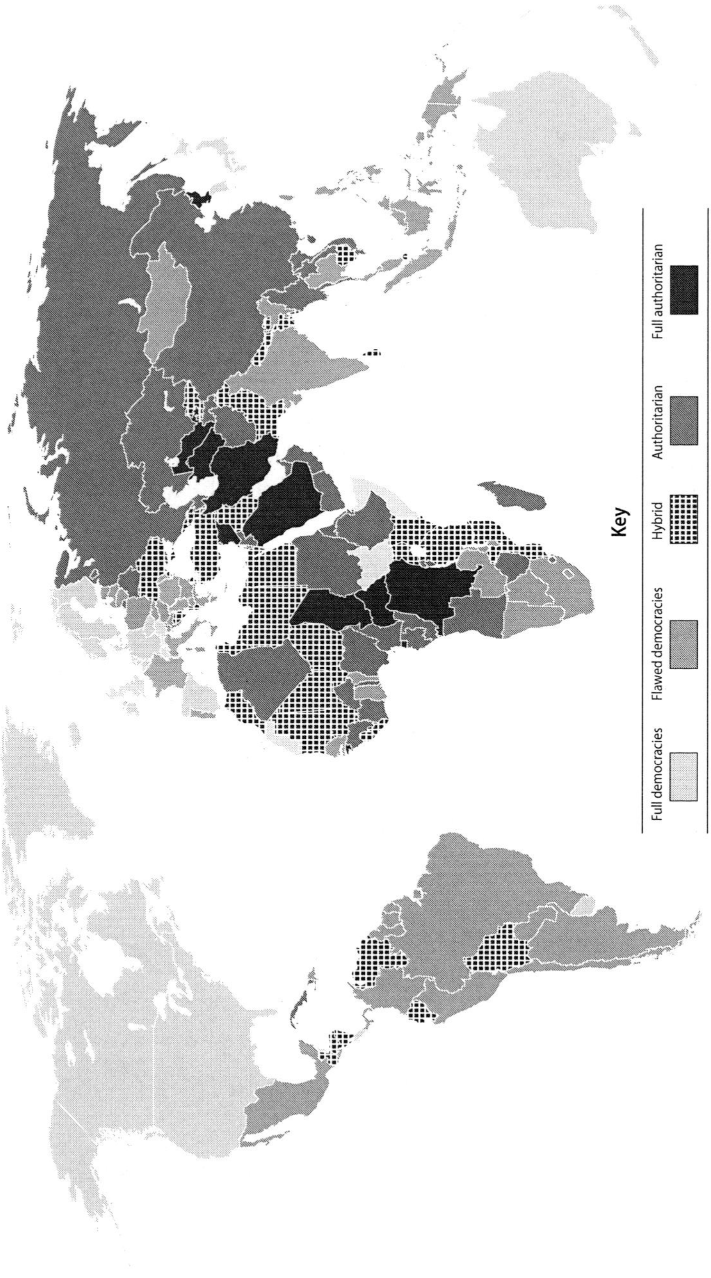

Governments come in many different forms. Some types of government give the citizens better representation and more freedom than others. The most democratic governments give all power to the citizens and provide many freedoms and liberties. Limited democratic governments give less representation and limit citizens' freedoms. An <u>authoritarian</u> government is one that controls the people and gives little or no representation and few freedoms to citizens.

The democracy index ranks the countries of the world from most democratic to least democratic. When deciding a country's rank, the democracy index considers the country's election process, citizens' rights and freedoms, government structure, and political participation by citizens.

---

1. A. What information is given by this map?
   B. Which category best describes the map—topographical, political, or special purpose? Explain your answer.
2. According to the text, what four factors affect how democratic a country is?
3. A. Use the text to define <u>authoritarian</u>.
   B. **True** or **false**: Authoritarian governments are the most democratic. Explain your answer.
4. Most governments in South America are classified into which group?
5. A "hybrid" is a mixture combining two different elements. What two elements are mixed in the hybrid governments on the map?
6. Which continent includes governments of all ranks?
7. A. According to the map, in what regions of the world are most authoritarian governments located?
   B. What can you infer about the freedoms and representations of people in those regions?
8. Cuba (the island below Florida) and China both have communist governments. What can you infer about the rights of citizens in these countries?

Systems of Government

Read the text and answer the questions.

National governments can be organized in three general ways. Each of the three systems of government describes how the government is organized and how much power is given to the national government.

In a unitary state, the national government controls all lower state and local governments. The national government decides what laws the state and local governments can and cannot make.

In a federation, a group of states join their powers together to form a strong national government. However, unlike a unitary state, individual states keep some freedoms, rights, and the ability to change the national government and make laws in their own states.

In a confederation, individual states join their powers together to form a weak national government. A confederation's central government provides support and protection for all the states, but gives far more power to the states.

PART A: Use the text to answer the questions.

1. Which system gives the least power to the national government?
2. Which system gives the most power to the national government?
3. Which system is a balance of power between state and national government?

PART B: Match each system of government underlined in the text to the graphic that represents it. Write the correct name under each picture.

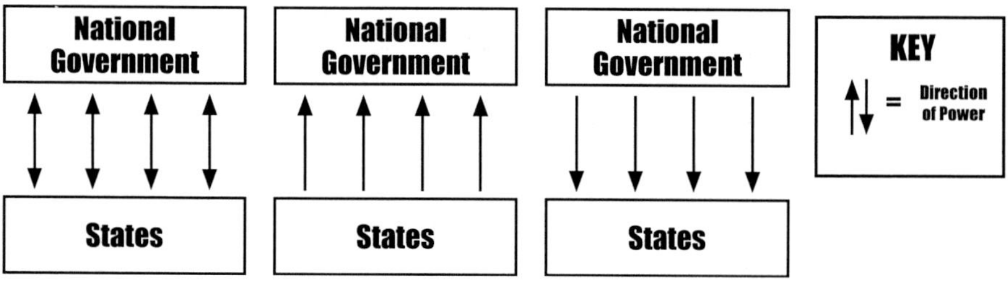

____________ ____________ ____________

PRIMARY SOURCE ANALYSIS

Name that Government!

Read each quote and complete parts A and B.

1) Mao Zedong: "Political power grows out of the barrel of a gun."

2) Henry David Thoreau: "That government is best which governs least."

3) Henry Clay: "Government is a trust, and the officers of the government are the trustees. And both the trust and trustees are created for the benefit of the people."

4) Andrew Jackson: "It is to be regretted that the rich and powerful too often bend the acts of government to their own selfish purposes."

5) Johann Wolfgang von Goethe: "The best government is that which teaches us to govern ourselves."

6) John I of England: "It is treason [for citizens] to dispute what a king may do..."

PART A: Match the letters of the quotes with the name of the form of government it represents.

________ anarchy ________ oligarchy

________ dictatorship ________ representative democracy

________ monarchy ________ democracy

PART B: Write the form of government represented by each image.

________________ ________________ ________________

Correlations to Common Core State Standards

For your convenience, correlations are listed page-by-page, and for the entire book!

This book is correlated to the Common Core State Standards for English Language Arts grades 3-8, and to Common Core State Standards for Literacy in History, Science, & Technological Subjects grades 6-8.

Correlations are highlighted in gray.

PAGE #	READING *Includes:* RI: Reading Informational Text RH: Reading History/Social Studies	WRITING *Includes:* W: Writing WHST: Writing History/Social Studies, Science, & Technical Subjects	LANGUAGE *Includes:* L: Language LF: Language Foundational Skills	SPEAKING & LISTENING *Includes:* SL: Speaking & Listening
2	RI RH . **1** **2** 3 **4** **5** 6 7 **8** 9 **10**	W WHST . 1 **2** 3 **4** 5 6 7 8 9 **10**	L LF . 1 2 3 **4** 5 6	SL . 1 2 3 4 5 6
3	RI RH . **1** **2** **3** **4** **5** 6 7 **8** 9 **10**	W WHST . 1 **2** 3 **4** 5 6 7 8 9 10	L LF . 1 2 3 **4** 5 **6**	SL . 1 2 3 4 5 6
4-5	RI RH . **1** **2** 3 **4** **5** **6** **7** **8** **9** **10**	W WHST . 1 **2** **3** **4** **5** 6 7 **8** **9** **10**	L LF . 1 2 **3** **4** **5** **6**	SL . 1 2 3 4 5 6
6	RI RH . **1** **2** **3** **4** **5** 6 7 **8** **9** **10**	W WHST . 1 **2** 3 **4** 5 6 7 **8** **9** **10**	L LF . 1 2 3 **4** **5** **6**	SL . 1 2 3 4 5 6
7	RI RH . **1** **2** 3 **4** **5** 6 7 8 **9** **10**	W WHST . 1 **2** 3 **4** 5 6 7 **8** **9** **10**	L LF . 1 2 3 **4** 5 **6**	SL . 1 2 3 4 5 6
8	RI RH . **1** **2** **3** **4** **5** 6 **7** **8** **9** **10**	W WHST . 1 **2** 3 **4** 5 6 7 **8** **9** **10**	L LF . 1 2 3 **4** 5 **6**	SL . 1 2 3 4 5 6
9	RI RH . 1 **2** **3** **4** 5 **6** 7 8 **9** **10**	W WHST . **1** **2** 3 **4** 5 6 7 8 **9** **10**	L LF . 1 2 **3** **4** 5 6	SL . 1 2 3 4 5 6
10	RI RH . **1** **2** **3** **4** **5** **6** **7** **8** **9** **10**	W WHST . 1 **2** **3** **4** **5** 6 7 **8** **9** **10**	L LF . 1 **2** **3** **4** **5** **6**	SL . **1** **2** 3 **4** 5 6
11	RI RH . **1** **2** 3 **4** **5** 6 7 **8** 9 **10**	W WHST . 1 **2** 3 **4** 5 6 7 8 **9** **10**	L LF . 1 2 3 **4** **5** **6**	SL . 1 2 3 4 5 6
12-13	RI RH . 1 2 3 4 **5** 6 **7** **8** 9 **10**	W WHST . 1 2 3 4 5 6 **7** **8** 9 **10**	L LF . 1 2 3 **4** 5 6	SL . 1 2 3 4 5 6
14	RI RH . **1** **2** 3 **4** **5** 6 7 **8** **9** **10**	W WHST . 1 **2** 3 **4** 5 6 7 **8** 9 **10**	L LF . 1 2 3 **4** 5 **6**	SL . 1 2 3 4 5 6
15	RI RH . **1** **2** **3** 4 **5** **6** 7 **8** **9** **10**	W WHST . 1 **2** 3 **4** **5** **6** **7** **8** 9 **10**	L LF . 1 2 3 **4** **5** **6**	SL . **1** **2** 3 **4** **5** **6**
16	RI RH . **1** **2** **3** **4** **5** 6 7 **8** 9 **10**	W WHST . 1 **2** 3 **4** **5** 6 7 8 **9** **10**	L LF . 1 2 3 **4** 5 **6**	SL . 1 2 3 4 5 6
17	RI RH . **1** **2** **3** **4** **5** 6 7 **8** 9 **10**	W WHST . 1 **2** 3 **4** 5 6 7 **8** **9** **10**	L LF . 1 2 **3** **4** **5** **6**	SL . 1 2 3 4 5 6
18	RI RH . **1** **2** **3** **4** **5** **6** **7** **8** **9** **10**	W WHST . **1** **2** 3 **4** **5** 6 7 **8** **9** **10**	L LF . 1 2 3 **4** **5** **6**	SL . **1** **2** 3 4 5 **6**
19	RI RH . **1** **2** 3 **4** **5** 6 7 8 **9** **10**	W WHST . 1 **2** 3 **4** 5 6 7 8 9 **10**	L LF . 1 2 3 **4** 5 **6**	SL . 1 2 3 4 5 6
20-21	RI RH . **1** **2** **3** **4** **5** 6 **7** 8 **9** **10**	W WHST . 1 **2** 3 **4** 5 6 **7** **8** **9** **10**	L LF . 1 2 3 **4** **5** **6**	SL . 1 2 3 4 5 6
22	RI RH . **1** 2 **3** **4** **5** 6 **7** 8 9 **10**	W WHST . 1 2 3 4 5 6 7 8 9 10	L LF . 1 2 3 **4** 5 **6**	SL . 1 2 3 4 5 6
23	RI RH . 1 **2** 3 **4** 5 6 **7** 8 **9** **10**	W WHST . 1 2 3 4 5 6 7 8 9 10	L LF . 1 2 3 **4** 5 **6**	SL . 1 2 3 4 5 6
COMPLETE BOOK	RI RH . **1** **2** **3** **4** **5** **6** **7** **8** **9** **10**	W WHST . **1** **2** **3** **4** **5** **6** **7** **8** **9** **10**	L LF . 1 2 **3** **4** **5** **6**	SL . **1** **2** 3 **4** **5** **6**

For the complete Common Core standard identifier, combine your grade + "." + letter code above + "." + number code above.

In addition to the correlations indicated here, the activities may be adapted or expanded to align to additional standards and to meet the diverse needs of your unique students!